COLUMBUS

Other books by Ingri & Edgar Parin d' Aulaire

ABRAHAM LINCOLN

BENJAMIN FRANKLIN

BUFFALO BILL

GEORGE WASHINGTON

LEIF THE LUCKY

POCAHONTAS

Published by Beautiful Feet Books
1306 Mill Street
San Luis Obispo, CA 93401

www.bfbooks.com
800.889.1978

For Nicolas Martin

COLUMBUS

INGRI & EDGAR
PARIN D'AULAIRE

Published by Beautiful Feet Books

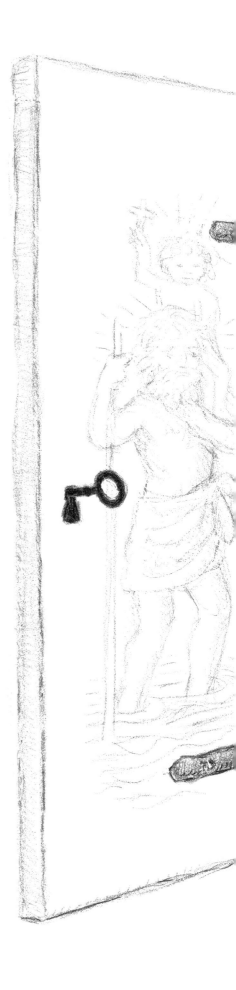

There once was a boy

who loved the salty sea.

He would be a seaman when he grew up.

He would not be a weaver like his father,

who sat all day

in a dark, little shop

weaving yarn into cloth.

A ship would be his shuttle,

the waves his warp,

4   the wide and bounding sea his loom.

He was a strong and tall boy with fiery blue eyes and reddish-blond
hair. His name was Christopher Columbus.

He was born in Italy, in the seaport of Genoa, more than 500 years ago. Christopher liked to listen to the loud talk of the sailors who walked in and out of the city gate, close by his father's house. He heard their tales about storms and adventures at sea and faraway lands, almost at the end of the world.

6

For in those days most people thought that if you sailed far enough
out into the ocean you would come to the end of the world. They still
thought that the world was flat as a platter. They laughed at the learned
men who said that the world was not small and flat but a huge ball that
spun around in space.

Once, when Christopher held an orange in his hand, he saw the tips of a butterfly's wings peeping up from behind it. He thought that just like this did the sails of a ship, far away, rise slowly over the horizon. It must be true that the world was round!

But when he said this to the other boys who were sailing and playing with him on the long, pebbly beaches outside of town, they all laughed. Then the people in India and China, at the other end of the world, must be walking upside down like flies on a ceiling, they giggled. Christopher did not like to be laughed at. He was a serious boy and laughed little himself. He found it was better to keep his thoughts to himself, and let the other boys admire his strength and his skill at handling a boat. He got most of his schooling while he played and sailed with the other Genoese boys. But he also learned some Latin and navigation, so he could find his way in the open sea with the compass, the sun, and the stars.

With his two younger brothers as crew he sailed up and down the
Genoese coast and delivered the goods his father had woven.

When Christopher was thirteen, he left his father's house and sailed out into the world to seek his fortune as a seaman. He felt free as the gulls as he saw his native town fade out of sight. Soon he rose above his shipmates, for he was clever and capable and could make others carry out his orders. He was still a very young man when he became captain of a ship. For many years he busily sailed his ship back and forth across the Mediterranean Sea and had little time to wonder whether the world was round or flat, small or big. There were known lands and harbors all around this sea, and in the middle lay Italy, his native land, like a big boot. He fought the Moorish pirates and storms at sea, and he did not know what fear was. It was easy for him to get a crew. The sailors knew that here was a captain with bone in his nose, who always brought his ship safely back to port.

One day it happened that he took on board a cargo for faraway England. And so Christopher left the sea he knew so well and set off into the great Western Ocean, the unknown and boundless Atlantic.

Safely he passed through the Strait of Gibraltar. Safely he skirted the Spanish coast. But when he reached the Portuguese shore, a fleet of pirate ships bore down on him from behind a rocky point. Christopher would rather give up his life than surrender his ship. He fought. But there were too many against him, and his ship was sent to the bottom.

Luck was with Christopher Columbus. As he came up from the depths he saw an oar floating on the water. Just then the sun set and darkness hid him from the pirates. He swam and floated on the oar until he reached the shore. Bleeding and worn, he crawled up on land and there on his knees he thanked the Lord for saving him. His ship and all that he owned in the world were at the bottom of the sea. But in Portugal no able-bodied seaman needed to go begging. Columbus soon found work on a Portuguese ship and saw that God had arranged everything for the best. For Portugal in those days was the biggest sea power in the world. Its captains were sailing their ships ever farther to the north and to the south, to find new lands and new trade routes. The known world became bigger and bigger. They searched eagerly for the seaway to China and India, the rich fairy-tale lands of the Far East where the gates were said to be built of pearls and the houses shingled with gold. For the captain who could find his way to these shores and return, his ship loaded with fragrant spices and treasures of the

East, would be the richest and mightiest seaman in the world.

Christopher sailed north and south on Portuguese ships. He learned much, and again he rose fast in the ranks. Portugal was a country after his heart. He soon spoke the language like a native, and when he married a lady from Madeira he was looked upon as a Portuguese. She was a lady of high birth. Columbus was a handsome man with a stately bearing. He looked like a nobleman, and before long he was considered by everybody a Portuguese gentleman of the sea. Soon he even forgot that he was only the son of a humble weaver. But he did not forget to provide well for his old father, and he sent for his two younger brothers to come and make their fortunes in Portugal too.

In Portugal no one doubted that the world was round. Map makers and geographers sat in their shops making globes in different sizes and shapes. Some of them were shaped like pears, others were oblong like eggs, still others were round like balls. Columbus eagerly studied all these globes. As he studied them, he was struck by a new thought. Since the world was round, the East and West must meet somewhere. Maybe he could sail to the West and reach the East. But was the Atlantic Ocean too vast to be crossed? And were there winds out at sea to fill the sails of a ship? And were there really lands on the other side?

By his own free will, no sailor as yet had sailed out beyond the last outlying islands and rocks. But there were rumors of sailors, carried off by storms, who had sighted land far, far to the west. Wherever Columbus sailed he listened to stories about the Atlantic Ocean.

Far north in fog and darkness lay the island of Iceland. Here, under black mountains belching smoke and fire, the stories of the great seafarers, the Vikings, were passed down from father to son. An Icelander told Columbus the saga of Leif Erikson. Whether Columbus heard this story in Iceland or in England, nobody knows for certain.

At the time when the first Christian king ruled Norway, he sent Leif Erikson off to carry the Faith to the Norsemen on Greenland, for they were still heathens. Leif wanted to do what no other sailor had done before him. He sailed straight west across the ocean to reach Greenland without landing on the way. For weeks a great storm tossed his ship about. He missed Greenland, but he came to a strange coast, still farther west, on the other side of the ocean. This unknown land was fair. The Norsemen wanted to settle there, but fierce, dark-skinned natives drove the Vikings off.

Five centuries had passed, and now the way to these lands had been forgotten. But Leif Erikson's saga had been written down.

When Columbus heard this story, a fire was lit in him that was never to be extinguished. Now he was sure that the western ocean could be crossed and that there were lands on the far side. These lands must be part of Asia, for no one had ever heard of other continents than Europe, Africa, and Asia.

He also began to think that the Lord had chosen him to sail west across the sea to find the riches of the East for himself and to carry the Christian faith to the heathens. His name was Christopher. Had not the Lord chosen his name-saint, Saint Christopher, to carry the Christ Child across the dark water of a river? He must have ships, he must have men, to sail west to reach the East. He must find a king to be his patron.

The King of Portugal was a mighty prince with many ships at his command. Columbus went to him and asked him for ships and men. He would sail west and find the way to the East for Portugal. The country would flourish and so would the King. The King called in his advisers. For long years they kept Columbus waiting while they quibbled and argued. Some of them said the ocean was too vast to be crossed. Some said it might perhaps be possible to sail down the sea toward the setting sun, but how could a ship climb up the watery hill and get home again? At last they all agreed it could not be done, since it had never been done before.

As for the King, he thought that Columbus's demands were quite immoderate. For Columbus wanted huge rewards if he succeeded.

So Columbus had to look for another king to be his patron. He had lost his wife, but he had a little son. With him he set off for Spain. There ruled a king with a queen at his side, who was known for her virtue and wisdom.

King Ferdinand and Queen Isabella of Spain welcomed Columbus, for they wanted Spain to be mightier than Portugal. The good Queen Isabella also wanted to share her Christian faith with the people in the East who had never heard about Christ. But the King and Queen had their hands full fighting the heathen Moors, who were holding part of their kingdom. Their royal treasury was empty.

And they thought, too, that Columbus asked rather much for himself. Columbus was told to bide his time until the Moors were driven out of the Kingdom of Spain.

For seven more years Columbus waited. He saw his money dwindle, and when his purse was quite empty, he had to go begging for food for himself and his son.

On a dreary night he came to a little cloister, far out on the Spanish coast, where a red-tinted river falls into the wide, blue Atlantic Ocean. It was La Rabida Cloister. Seven kind monks lived there, and they welcomed Columbus and his son with open arms. There Columbus found a haven. In the quiet of the cloister he finished his plans for his voyage across the sea. The monks helped him. They asked the Queen's priest, who was a friend of theirs, to put in a good word for Columbus whenever he could. And when at last the Moorish stronghold, Granada, fell to the Spaniards, the priest sent word to the cloister for Columbus to come at once. The monks lent Columbus a mule, and hurriedly he rode off to

Granada.

Columbus found King Ferdinand and Queen Isabella in high good spirits in the royal camp outside the fallen citadel. The heathens had been driven out of Spain, and in their joy the King and Queen said yes to all of Columbus's demands. If he succeeded, they would make him admiral of the Ocean Sea and viceroy of all the lands he might claim for Spain, and grant him a share of all the riches he might find. The Queen was so eager to have him go, she would have sold her jewels, if need had been, to get money for ships for him. But now there was enough money in the royal treasury.

They gave him three ships and food and supplies for many months at sea. The Queen promised a large reward to the sailor who first sighted land. And the King gave Columbus a letter of greeting to his "Royal Brother," the Emperor of China.

Close by La Rabida Cloister lay the little port of Palos. There Columbus fitted out his ships and gathered his crews. It was difficult. For who sails lightheartedly into the unknown? But with much persuasion and great promises of treasure, Columbus found enough tough and adventurous sailors to man his three ships. He named them the *Niña*, the *Pinta*, and the *Santa Maria*. All three were small ships. The *Niña* was the smallest, only fifty feet long. The *Pinta* was the fastest. The *Santa Maria* was the largest, almost eighty feet long, over all. Columbus would sail on her.

Before dawn on Friday, August 3, 1492, Columbus led his men to church. They prayed for a safe and prosperous voyage, and his men vowed, with hands on the Bible, to follow his commands. Then they boarded the ships. The early-morning breeze swelled the sails. The outgoing tide carried the three little ships swiftly out of the Red River and into the long,

pale breakers of the Atlantic. The monks, with Columbus's young son at their side, stood at the cloister and blessed the expedition. Weeping women and children ran along the shore, wringing their hands in despair. They never expected to see their fathers and husbands again.

The church bells tolled.

At first the sailors were boisterous and gay. They were the men who dared to sail where no one had sailed before. And they would return with gold and treasures from the East.

But when they had sailed out beyond the Canary Islands and into the vast ocean, where even the birds from the outlying rocks could follow them no longer, they began to worry. There was nothing before them and nothing behind them but sea and sky. One day was like another. Calm and alone, in command of his ships, Columbus stood on the poop deck of the *Santa Maria*. He trusted no one but himself. He could hardly sleep or rest.

"To the west, helmsman," he called, "not to the north, not to the south, not to the east, but straight to the west."

He watched the stars; he checked his maps and his compass and kept his ships on a steady course. He wrote two logbooks. One he kept hidden. There he wrote, day by day, how many miles they had sailed by his reckoning. The other logbook he showed to his men. There the distances from home appeared much shorter, to soothe their worries.

Each day that passed, the sailors worried more and grumbled louder. Not only were they afraid of the unknown sea, but also their water turned stale, their food turned rancid.

"Oh, for a bunch of fresh grapes, a piece of juicy meat, a drink from the sweet well at home," they sighed. All day long they wished for nothing better than to return to Spain.

Columbus kept their spirits up through his lonely, iron will. "West to the West," he repeated. For three weeks they sailed before the wind. The wind was gentle, the sea so smooth, it was like sailing on a river. Seaweed began to appear all around them, until the water was covered with it as far as they could see. It looked as if the ships were sitting in a field. The winds died; the sails hung limp.

The sailors were terrified. They thought that now they were stuck forever in a floating meadow. Still greater was their terror when all the flying and crawling bugs on board disappeared as if by magic. And when they saw that the needle of the compass quivered strangely and did not point to the North Star, they wrung their hands and begged the Lord to have mercy on their souls. Columbus had to step down from his deck to cheer up his men. He walked among them and showed them that the weeds were not growing from the bottom of the sea. There was only a thick layer on the surface. As for the fleas and flies which had bothered them for so long, they should only be glad to be rid of them, he said. Why the compass behaved so queerly he could not say, for that he did not know.

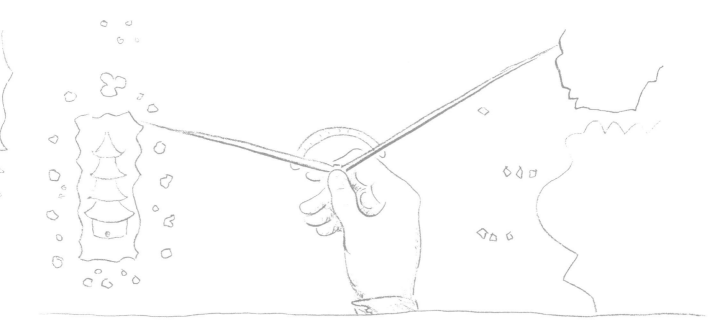

At last a soft wind rippled the sails, and the ships moved slowly ahead through the sea of weeds. But now the sailors had lost all courage. They begged Columbus to turn about and sail back to Spain. They threatened to throw him into the sea and take over the ships. Had they but known the way back home without him, they would have done it. They had to follow his command and continue on to the West. To cheer them, he said they would not have much farther to sail, and told them to think of the riches that were waiting. Again their spirits rose. The sea was changing, and so was the mood of the sailors.

Then his men began crying "Land" whenever they saw low clouds. They cheered and shouted for joy, but when Columbus showed them that they were mistaken, they were gloomier than ever. At last Columbus lost his patience. He proclaimed that any man who again cried "Land" falsely would not get his reward even were he to see real land later.

Days went by; weeks went by. They sailed on and on and saw nothing but the desolate sea and sky. At last, one day, they spied a strange object in the water. It was a carved stick. Soon afterward a sailor fished up a branch with buds and flowers. The salty air seemed sweet and fragrant in their nostrils, as if scented already by the spices of India. Next day great flocks of land birds flew over the masts. Land must be near. For the first time Columbus changed his command. He called, "To the southwest," and followed the birds.

Now every man was peering ahead.

Late at night, while Columbus stood at his lonely watch, staring through the dark, it seemed to him that one of the stars, low in the sky, looked different from the others. It didn't twinkle. It flickered like the flame of a candle. It could not be a star. It must be a fire kindled by man.

Columbus called his men. They all saw it. He ordered the anchors dropped so the ships would not hit a reef in the night. Before dawn a cannon shot boomed. It was a signal from the *Pinta,* which was ahead. Her crew had seen breakers and a dark coast line.

32   It was Friday, October 12, 1492.

In the pearly gray light of dawn Columbus glimpsed a low coast, half hidden in the spray of the surf. As the sun rose over the crystal-clear emerald water, he saw a lovely, green island. A chorus of sweet-singing and chattering birds filled the air. It was like reaching paradise, after the ten bleak weeks at sea.

With the letter for the Emperor of China in his hand, Columbus went ashore, followed by his men. He stuck the Holy Cross and the banner of Spain into the glistening sand and claimed the land for the Spanish crown. Then he fell to his knees with all his men and thanked the Lord for having brought them safely to this island off the Indian coast.

But where were the golden towers and where were the pearly gates? And where were the richly clad ambassadors who would lead him to their prince? All he could see were naked, red-skinned savages. They threw themselves to the ground and worshiped Columbus and his bearded men. The natives had never seen white men or sails before. They thought that gods had descended from the heavens on white-winged birds. They led the white gods to their homes in the shady, green jungle and eagerly set before them a feast. Hungrily Columbus and his men seized the tropical fruits and strange foods offered to them. The Spaniards did not mind being treated like gods by these gentle heathens to whom they had come to bring the Christian faith. They lay down on the grass and rested, surrounded by cool springs and marvelous flowers.

These natives did not have yellow skin and slanting eyes. Columbus knew they could not be Chinese, so what else could they be but Indians? They called their island Guanahani. (Columbus named it San Salvador.)

34

Dewdrops glistened like pearls, and the bright feathers of parrots sparkled like rubies and emeralds among the leaves. But these were not the kind of treasure that could be gathered by gold-greedy men. The only real gold that gleamed was in the little nose ornaments the Indians wore. These they gladly gave to the white men in exchange for little red caps

and tinkling bells. Columbus asked the Indians in sign language from where this gold came. They pointed to the southwest. Then Columbus and his men hurried back to their ships and sailed on the way the Indians had pointed. Columbus passed many low, green islands. Some of them were so densely grown that not even a cat could have gotten ashore.

37

At other islands naked natives ran to the shores to worship the white men as gods. In return for their golden ornaments the sailors gave them any little things they could lay their hands on, even pieces of rope and broken dishes. For Columbus had forbidden them to take the natives' gold for nothing; he wanted their good will.

After the small, low islands, Columbus came to big islands, with sky-high mountains. He discovered Cuba, but when he found no gold there, he continued on to Haiti. The water was so clear and seemed so safe that Columbus relaxed his watch and lay down to rest. While he slept, the *Santa Maria* struck a coral reef in a shallow bay and was wrecked. Columbus could not save his ship; the *Santa Maria* broke to pieces. Indians came paddling out to help the white gods who were in distress, and they brought ashore everything from the wreck that could be moved.

At first Columbus was downcast and sad. But soon he was cheered, for on Haiti there was gold. The innocent Indians told him there was gold in the mountains. Again Columbus marveled at how God had arranged everything for the best. He had lost his ship, but he had gained a gold mine for Spain.

Now he would sail home on the *Niña* to get more ships. Some of them would carry back to Spain the gold from the mines. Others he would use to sail on to the mainland of Asia.

Out of the timbers of the *Santa Maria* he built a fort on shore. There he left some of his men to watch over the gold mines and over Haiti, which he named Hispaniola. But the men he left behind were greedy and cruel. The Indians soon understood that these were no gods but heartless men who cared only for gold.

Roaring gales blew Columbus swiftly homeward across the ocean. The waves ran mountain-high and water broke over the decks in torrents of white foam. Columbus feared the ships would go down and the world would never know of his discoveries, so he wrote a report of his voyage and put it in a barrel. Then he sealed the barrel tightly and tossed it overboard. He hoped that somewhere, sometime, it would be found. Then the sea calmed down, and Columbus himself reached Spain safely. Nobody knows what ever became of the barrel.

Great was the joy in Palos when the *Niña* and the *Pinta* came sailing into port. The King and Queen were far up north in their kingdom. Columbus at once set off to reach them. He took along with him samples of all he had found on his voyage. He had gaily plumed parrots, strange fruits and sweet-smelling herbs, and a small chest filled with golden ornaments. He had even brought along some Indians to show. They shivered and froze in the brisk air of Spain. Proudly Columbus led his little procession through the country. Whenever he came to a village or town he took the gold out of the chest and hung it all over the Indians. People came out from castles and caves to marvel at such splendor and to admire Columbus. With the riches of the East almost at his feet, every Spaniard now saw himself as a rich and mighty lord. Columbus was the hero of Spain. The word of his triumphant return traveled ahead of him. The King and the Queen themselves came riding out to meet him. Too late the King of Portugal was sorry he had turned him away.

The Queen clasped her hands with joy when Columbus showed the treasures he had brought home and told about the wonderful Indian islands. Even the proud king looked pleased. The crew of the *Pinta* claimed the reward for first seeing land, but the Queen ruled that Columbus should have it himself. For it was he who had first seen the light. Now

Columbus was happy. All his dreams had come true. The King and Queen
showered him with honors. He was made a grandee of Spain, admiral of
the Ocean Sea, and viceroy of Hispaniola. A fleet of seventeen ships was
made ready for him so he could sail still farther west and reach India and
China.

43

This time it was easy enough for Columbus to man his ships. The fifteen hundred men he needed were pushing and crowding each other to get on board. They all wanted to get rich fast, and women and children were urging them on. Also, Columbus's two brothers had come to sail with him. Flags were waving and trumpets were blaring as Columbus proudly led his fleet out to sea.

But when he made his landfall on the other side of the ocean, he found no rich islands and no friendly Indians. He came to Dominica and to nearby Guadeloupe. These islands were so wild and steep, it seemed as if the waterfalls came tumbling out of the clouds. The Indians who lived there were wild too. They were cannibals who ate their enemies. They had no riches of any kind and received the white men with poisoned darts.

Columbus and his men were very disappointed, so he led his fleet on. He found many beautiful islands, but he found neither Asia nor gold, and his men grew very impatient. When they came to Hispaniola and found the fortress in ruins and not a Spaniard left to tell the tale, their impatience changed to anger against Columbus.

The Indians had run away and were hiding in the jungles. The Spaniards hunted them and made them their slaves. They forced them to build fortresses and towns and to toil in the gold mines.

The queen had ruled that the Indians were to be treated kindly and only gently converted to Christianity. When Columbus reminded his men of this, they refused to obey and began to plot against him. Columbus, who handled his men so well at sea, could not handle them on land.

When he returned to Spain to ask for still more ships to continue his search, the King and Queen received him coldly. Evil tongues had whispered into their ears that Columbus wanted to make himself king over the Indian islands.

Columbus talked himself back into favor at court, for he was a good talker. And the King and the Queen gave him some ships so he could sail off for the third time. But in secrecy they sent a Spanish noble on another ship to Hispaniola. He was to judge if the rumors about Columbus were true. And no free Spaniard would sail with Columbus now. For crews he had to take bad men out of prison.

On his third voyage Columbus came to the mouth of the Orinoco River on the South American continent. He could tell that he had reached a continent, for the river was so large that its fresh water sweetened the ocean all around it. But it was an unknown continent. Columbus had no use for it. It barred his way to Asia. Columbus was puzzled; his men were rebellious. A violent fever racked his body. He gave up his search and sailed again for Hispaniola. There the Spanish noble was waiting for him. He planned to be viceroy himself, and had joined the men who were plotting against Columbus. He arrested Columbus as a traitor to Spain and put him in chains. His brothers and faithful men wanted to fight to free him. But Columbus said no. His pride was hurt. Only the King and Queen themselves could set him free and restore his honor.

The chains rattled, the storms shrieked as Columbus was shipped as a prisoner back across the ocean. His hair had turned white, but the fire was still in his eyes.

46

In proud silence Columbus approached the King and Queen, his heavy chains dragging behind him. The King and Queen were embarrassed and ordered his chains removed. They treated Columbus kindly and punished the plotting grandee, but they made another man viceroy of Hispaniola in his stead. Maybe they did not feel themselves bound by their promises as long as Columbus had not reached the Far East and delivered the King's letter to the Emperor of China.

Columbus had to have ships and sail off once more to find a passage through the unknown continent he had found. He was still sure that Asia must lie right behind it. He would deliver the letter to the Emperor of China, and all his honors would be restored.

He had to wait for a long time. At last he was given four old and worm-eaten ships. Columbus, too, was getting old and full of aches and pains.

On his fourth voyage Columbus sailed on to the west, past Hispaniola, until he came to the long coast of Central America. It was the hurricane season, and storms such as no Spaniard had ever seen tossed his poor old ships about until they leaked in every joint. Winds lashed with such fury that the water was seething like a pot on a hot fire. A waterspout approached the ships. It drew the water up to the clouds, twisting it about like a whirlwind. All the ships would have gone down if Columbus had not felt the oncoming storms in his aching joints and made ready for them in time. But sometimes his pains grew so bad that he couldn't stand up. Then he had his bed brought out on deck and directed his ships from there. This time his son sailed with him. He stood at his father's side and was his biggest comfort.

When the sea was calm, millions of mosquitoes swarmed out from the jungles. The poisonous stings made the white men feverish and their skins turned yellow, as in mockery of the yellow gold they yearned for and did not find.

Columbus sailed up and down the endless coast, looking for an opening. He found no passage through the land, for there was none. And he never found the enormous Indian treasures hidden behind the tangled jungles. Time was running short. The worms in the warm, tropical waters ate their way ever deeper into his rotting ships. He had to abandon one ship. With the others he set off across the Caribbean Sea, hoping to reach Hispaniola before they sank. But on the way water began to leak in faster than his men could pump it out. Slowly his ships were sinking. He had to sail them up on a beach on the lonely island of Jamaica. There stood the riddled, old ships, side by side on the white sand. They would never again be afloat, and no ship would ever sail by and come to rescue the shipwrecked men. Was the great Columbus going to pine away on this faraway island?

Two of his men set off in a frail canoe to try to brave the treacherous sea and bring help from Hispaniola. But the sea was full of currents and Hispaniola was more than a hundred miles away. Their chances of getting across were small.

Soon all the food on board the three ships was eaten. The Indians of the island were friendly, and for a while they came with food. But before long they were all worn out feeding the hungry sailors, who ate as much in one meal as they themselves ate in a week. The Indians ate little and worked little. They refused to bring the white men any more food.

The marooned men were feeling the pangs of hunger, when one day Columbus saw from his observations that soon there would be a full eclipse of the moon. The crafty Columbus could turn an eclipse of the moon to his advantage. He sent word to the Indians that his God was angry with them for letting the white men starve. Now he would punish them and take their moon away.

When night came and the moon slowly grew smaller and smaller, the Indians trembled. They ran to Columbus and promised to bring him food if they could have the moon back. Columbus said he would plead in their favor. He stood on deck and made magic signs until the eclipse had passed.

Again the moon shone brightly over the island. The shipwrecked men no longer starved, for now the Indians feared Columbus and his magic powers. For a year Columbus sat on the island. He had given up hope of ever being saved, when one day he saw the sails of two Spanish ships. The men in the canoe had really reached Hispaniola, and now they were returning to rescue Columbus and his men. The rescued men were happy, and so were the Indians, who did not have to feed them any longer.

In Hispaniola, Columbus collected his share of the gold from the mines. With his own gold he paid his men and bought a ship to take him home to Spain. He never again became viceroy over the lands he had found. But his son did later, in his stead.

Old and tired, Columbus returned to Spain from his fourth and last voyage. While he had been searching in vain, the Portuguese had found the seaway to the East by sailing south around Africa. Now Columbus stood in the shadow.

The rest of his days he spent at his home in Valladolid in Spain, wondering and pondering why he had not found the way to the East. He blamed the unknown continent that had barred his way. It never occurred to him to be grateful that the unknown American continent had been in his way. Otherwise he and his men would have starved to death on the endless way to Asia. For the world was three times as wide around as Columbus had believed.

Many people say that Columbus was poor and forsaken in his old age. That is not true. He wasn't poor, but he was bitter because he was not the richest and mightiest seaman in the world. Columbus was a great man. But he was not a modest man. He wanted too much, and so he did not get enough. While he lived nobody realized the full importance of his discoveries. Many other captains were sailing their ships across the Atlantic Ocean and no longer needed him to show them the way. The ocean was wide, but its eerie spell had been broken. People soon forgot that no one had dared to cross the Atlantic before Columbus had proved that it could be done. That irked the aging Columbus.

It is said that once in company he had a basket of eggs brought to his table. He asked those present to take an egg and set it upright on the table. They all tried. Eggs wobbled and rolled, and at last they agreed that it could not be done. But Columbus took an egg and set it down so firmly that the bottom cracked and flattened. The egg stood upright.

Then everybody cried out that they could all have done it too.

"Yes," said Columbus, "it is simple now that I have shown you how!"

In Genoa in Italy

there stands a gray, deserted house

squeezed in between an ancient city gate

and tall, modern buildings.

Its shutters are closed; its doors are bolted.

It has nothing to set it apart from other little old houses

except for a sign over its windows which says that

this house, more than any other, claims the right

to be the childhood home of Christopher Columbus.

From here the little boy set out into the world

to weave a lasting pattern on the trackless waste of the sea,

and to find, in the end, a new world

56   beyond the turbulent waters.